A SONG FOR LIV

A SONG FOR LIV

by Wayne Gudmundson

NDSU NORTH DAKOTA STATE
UNIVERSITY PRESS

Fargo, North Dakota

NDSU NORTH DAKOTA STATE
UNIVERSITY PRESS

Dept. 2360, P.O. Box 6050, Fargo, ND 58108-6050
www.ndsupress.org

A Song for Liv, by Wayne Gudmundson

First Edition
First Printing

Library of Congress Control Number: 2021934448
ISBN: 978-1-946163-32-5

Cover and interior photography by Wayne Gudmundson
Cover and interior design by Deb Tanner

The publication of *A Song for Liv* is made possible by the generous support of the Muriel and Joseph Richardson Fund, donors to the NDSU Press Fund and the NDSU Press Endowed Fund, and other contributors to NDSU Press.

David Bertolini, Director
Suzzanne Kelley, Publisher
Oliver West Sime, Graduate Assistant in Publishing

Book Team for *A Song for Liv*:
Abigail Keys and Elle West

Publisher's Cataloging-In-Publication Data available at Library of Congress

∞ This paper meets the requirements of ANSI/NISO Z39.48-1992
(Permanence of Paper).

Table of Contents

AFTERWORD

Acknowledgments

Appendix

Notes

About the Author

About the Press

This book is dedicated to Emile and Colette Gudmundson. This "song" now belongs to you.

PREFACE

This journey began years ago on family trips to visit my grandparents in the Icelandic community of Mountain, North Dakota. I first went to Iceland to make photographs in 1993 in an effort to locate the birthplace of a poet and in doing so became interested in finding some of my ancestral landscapes.

A Song for Liv slowly came into focus, not as a road map pointing a specific direction, but more like a jigsaw puzzle with successive pieces fitting together, offering a direction, but not following a chronological game plan.

The individual pieces or vignettes took shape in three parts, largely because of how I worked. The diary entries were an immediate response to the surroundings, the reflections were the result of my research and memory, and the photographs were a more visceral response to the place or the idea or feeling about the previous two components.

Wayne Gudmundson
Bad Medicine Lake, Minnesota

I. An Introduction

At the Funeral of . . .
I feel content that you would grin with me
Could you but witness what I hear and see.
For you were not accustomed—not your fate—
To be thus borne along by friends in state.

But death has changed your status, so that now
Your friends assemble in your honor, bow
Their heads in faith, in grief, humility,
And all unite in speaking well of thee!

Kristján Niels Julíus (K.N.)

An Introduction

As a four-year-old, I assumed that everyone was more or less like me. Perhaps their winter parkas had a different army green tint, or their buckle overshoes had four instead of five metal clasps, or their post–World War II rambler homes had three instead of two bedrooms.

My father grew up in an Icelandic community in northeastern North Dakota. The three-and-a-half-hour drive was a regular occurrence and the people and the events that took place there seemed to me to be quite regular—not unlike my overshoes.

I first went to Iceland on purpose in 1993 to find the birthplace of Kristján Niels Julíus, a poet who ended up on a farm near Mountain, North Dakota.

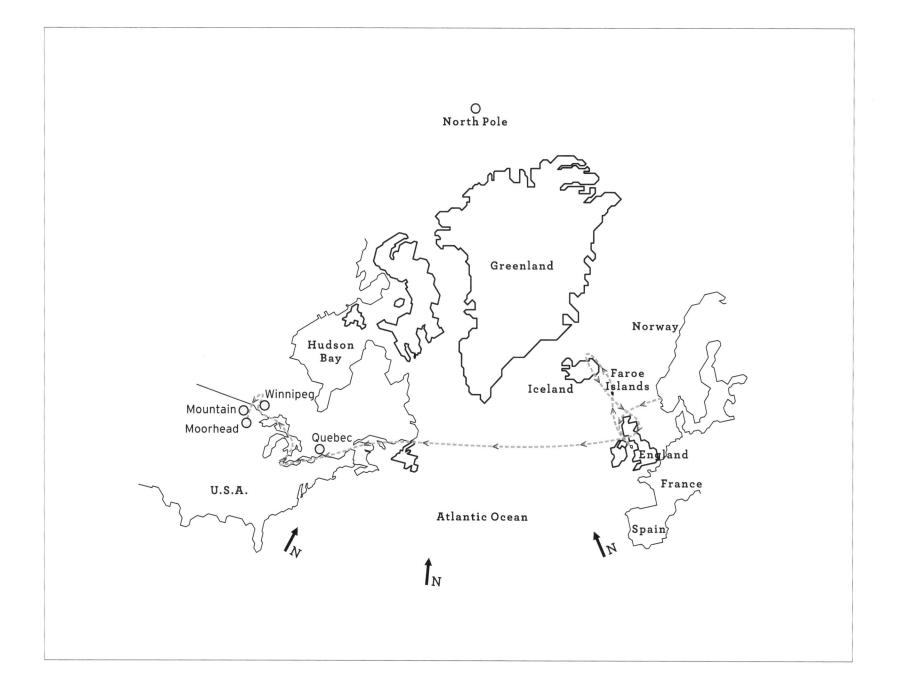

Mountain, North Dakota, 20 March 1987

The March sun feels good as my wife, Jane, and I drive toward Mountain. This will be our two-month-old daughter Liv's first visit to my Icelandic grandparents' home. We drive to the top of the hill just west of town and turn our little Datsun around. The view looking east into the Red River Valley is a familiar one, but its vastness still commands my attention.

. . .

Years ago, I was introduced to the North Dakota landscape as a child in the back seat of a 1954 red and white Chevy on family trips to visit my grandparents. With Fargo still visible over my shoulder, my brother, Curt, would ask, "How much farther?" My mother would sigh and without turning around say, "about 160 miles [the distance from Fargo to Mountain], and not until we pass the two white churches." After what seemed like years, the first white church finally came into view. There stubbornly stood Thingvalla Lutheran, facing west with the curious field stone monument just to its right with the bas-relief face of a man staring somberly back at it. "Who's that guy, Dad?" I'd ask. Smiling, no doubt because we are so close to Mountain, but also because of the memory, my Icelandic father would say, "Ahh . . . that's old K.N. [pronounced—cow-en]. He was a gravedigger, a handyman, and a poet."

Down the gully, over the small stream, left past the Borg old folks home, we finally made a sweeping right turn and looked up Main Street, Mountain. Even in the fifties, each trip back brought news of another business gone, another family moved, another death. But to a child, this was as interesting as the chemical makeup of the white paint on the pine boards of the other church, Vikur Lutheran, which sat next to my grandparents' house. As we would pull into their drive, we'd briefly see my grandmother's face in the kitchen window before she'd explode out the back door to greet us warmly with laughter and hugs.

Each visit would include a trip to the hill west of town. At the top, Grandpa Chris would turn the Chevy (later Fords) around and stop. After too much adult talk, he would say the magic words that we in the back seat were silently suffering to hear, "Well, how far do you think we can go?" Guesses made, brake off, clutch in—we were joyfully on our way.

. . .

After making a photo of the road vanishing into the valley, I get back into the warmth of the car and say to Jane, who now is holding our daughter, "Well, how far do you think we can go?" On this baptismal trip down the hill we coast past familiar landmarks and come to rest just short of the old town hall—a respectable effort. We drive down Main Street—no reason to stop—and head on out of town. What will Liv know of any of this, of all these ghosts? In his book, Songlines, *Bruce Chatwin wrote of the Australian Aborigines who mapped their land with songs that recorded not only places but personal events that were connected to those locations. He said that they believed that unless the songs were sung the land would die.*

4

Schroeder's Hill

South of Mountain, North Dakota, 1 August 1990

Sunny and dry. Bill Holm and I head north from Bad Medicine Lake in his battleship gray Ford Crown Victoria. I drive along the gravel road, and in the rearview mirror watch the dust lift off the surface like an expanding vapor trail. "Here, try this one," Bill says, handing me another type of beef jerky. Then he pushes the big, brown paper bag of goodies to the floor and pours two coffees. "For the K.N. book we'll need a couple of types of translations."

. . .

As a kid visiting my grandparents, we'd always stop at the farm of Arni and Rosa Johnson. After the usual greetings, the men and women would separate into their respective conversational groups. As a six-year-old I could find a welcome place in either camp, but I was drawn to the men, who, after dealing with the required weather and car issues, would begin a regular ritual. They would take turns reciting K.N.'s poems in Icelandic, at which point they might nod and while inhaling, say softly, "Yow, yow." Or, torn with laughter they would bellow, "Yow, that's a good one, but have you heard about the time K.N. was walking home and a Model T went by and splashed mud on him? He instantly made a poem against this fellow.
It went like this . . ."

Occasionally, certain poems were spoken in English for the young ones in the crowd who were brought up to be Americans and knew no Icelandic. I remember thinking then, that it would be OK to be a man—laughing with friends, speaking a mysterious language, reciting and enjoying poetry that poked fun at people, politicians, and the church.

. . .

Now, driving south around Winnipeg, after our weekend in Gimli, Manitoba, it's quiet in the car except for Bill rustling through the New York Times. *He hands me a lemon drop, picks up a manuscript he's working on and reads a couple of poems out loud. "I'm going to call it,* The Dead Get by With Everything," *he says. Maybe they do, I think.*

Arni and Rosa Johnson's

Akureyri, Iceland, 17 June 1993

8:00 AM, Icelandic Independence Day, shockingly clear. These negatives are going to be contrasty. My new friend, Guðmundur Ingolfsson, had warned me about staying in the city park, "The kids will be partying," he said. I did, they did. Another sleepless night, but then, no one seems to sleep here. It's only dark when you close your eyes. I expect that it's a response to the dark, sleepful winters.

* * *

This town was home to K.N., the poet who settled on a farm near Mountain, North Dakota. The town historian said his house was there at the extreme end of old Akureyri. After fourteen years there, his mom died, and he moved in with her brother somewhere on a farm south of town for the next four years before heading for the New World.

Guðmundur gave me a photo taken in the late 1800s by Sigfús Eymundsson of a group of emigrating Icelanders aboard a ship just offshore. The passengers were staring into the camera—souls about to be stolen—shocked, I expect, by both the new medium and the realization that they were underway, their decision to move, made.

Eymundsson was also an agent for the Allan Line, selling hundreds of one-way tickets to his countrymen. Was he aware that he might be letting the vital air out of the national balloon, or maybe he thought that he was easing the Malthusian pressure? No, seldom are there such grand understandings. In all likelihood, he was just another poor photographer paying for his visual vice with a lucrative part-time job.

* * *

Fishing boats are unloading their catch, and one is heading out as I drive east across the causeway.

K.N.'s birthplace, south end of old Akureyri

South of Akureyri, Iceland, 20 June 1993

1:30 AM, just back from finding K.N.'s farm sites, now sitting outside my tent, looking across the fjord to Akureyri in the soft dusk/dawn light. I made a few good photos today and found what I came to find. I pour a dram of single malt and lift my glass to Kristján Niels Julíus a.k.a. K.N. Skol.

• • •

As I got out of the car and started approaching the farmhouse around 10:00 PM, a young guy came out of a barn. "Do you know of an old poet who left here around 1880 named K.N. Július? He came from somewhere near here," I said. "Old K.N.? Of course. He worked at a farm about a mile up the valley on the other side of the river. But he spent all of his time at his mom's brother's place just there." He said pointing to a place I passed on the way in. "Do you know his writing?" I asked. "Everyone knows his poetry," he said. "After you finish taking your pictures, stop by the house and have something to eat."

So K.N. worked at one farm, hung out at another. In North Dakota, he lived at one farm and hung out in town. One country revered him and another tolerated him—a poet and a handyman, a surrogate grandfather, and a scallywag.

The day started in the library digging through microfiche files that the Mormons helped assemble listing yearly census records of all the region's farms. As I was walking out with my treasure map, I said hello to a couple coming up the stairs. I told them that they sounded American. They said, "Yes, we're from Seattle, but originally we came from a small Icelandic community in North Dakota called Mountain." "My grandfather was Chris Gudmundson," I told them. "Oh, then you're Eddy's son. Are you doing genealogical research?"

• • •

It's hard to sleep in this beautiful light. Looking at the date on my watch, I realize that tomorrow is the solstice. I remember that my great-grandfather's wife, Anna, was a child on a little island north of here on the Arctic Circle.

East of the farm where K.N. worked before emigration

II. The Land

"This strange blue colour seemed to embrace all the mysteries of distance, and she stood for a moment overwhelmed by the prospect of such infinity. It was as if she had come to the edge of the world.

"Father," she said in a perplexed and hesitating voice, "where are we?"
"We've crossed the heath," he replied. "That's the ocean."
"Isn't there anything on the other side, then?" she asked finally.

"The foreign countries are on the other side," replied her father, proud of being able to explain such a vista. "The countries that they talk about in books," he went on, "the kingdoms."

Independent People by Halldór Laxness

The Land

In finding K.N.'s birthplace and uncovering bits of his story, I began to see glimpses of my own. These expanded diary excerpts began as a way of tracking my travels and thoughts, but soon became pieces of a puzzle about my ancestral family.

It became a pursuit across Iceland, but for what, I was not sure.

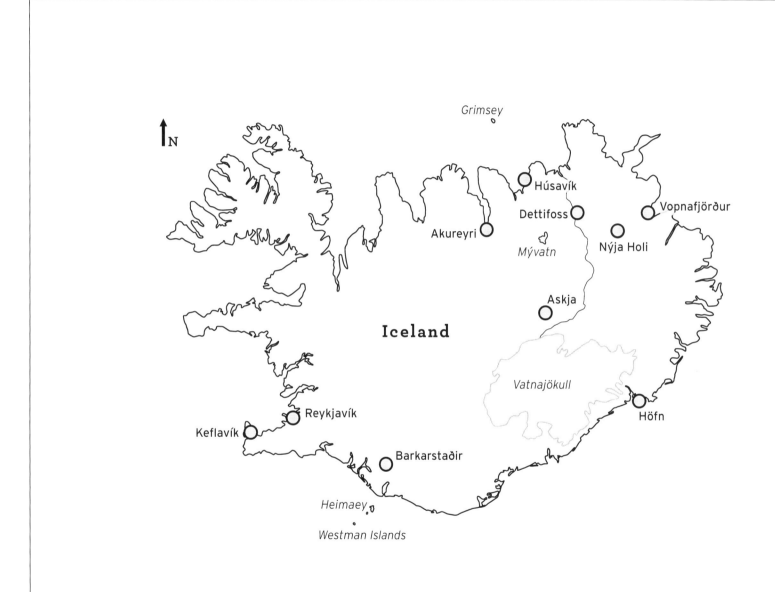

N

Grimsey

Húsavík

Dettifoss   Vopnafjörður

Akureyri   Nýja Holi

Mývatn

Iceland   Askja

Vatnajökull

Reykjavík   Höfn

Keflavík

Barkarstaðir

Heimaey

Westman Islands

Grímsey, Iceland, 21 June 1993

3:00 AM, clear, faint breeze from the Pole.

* * *

It was my great-grandparents Sigurbjörn and Anna who emigrated from Iceland and eventually settled in Mountain. Sigurbjörn came from a farm north of Húsavík and Anna lived in the Mývatn area, but for a time her family lived on this island—the most northerly in Iceland.

Here's an odd and perhaps cruel paradox: the old ones considered this island north of Iceland on the Arctic Circle to be Eden—grass for the sheep, some fish, gull eggs, and puffins for people to eat.

Anna's parents must have thought so too, as they moved here with her as an infant. Then, as the next three of her sisters were born, and successively died and were buried here as young children, they left this Eden—and their three little girls—and moved south to the main island.

* * *

Now, as I look north, time stops. Words stay away. This solstice vigil passes with the sounds of sheep munching grass, the regular flap of gulls' wings from the cliffs, and the intermittent cry of the terns. The sun arcs toward the horizon, then before it's allowed to define the end of one day, it begins the next.

Arctic Ocean looking north

North of Húsavík, Iceland, 29 June 1993

10:00 AM, a raw wind from the west, a raw light from the north. I wonder if that guy digging through the junkyard found anything. This is probably the best-looking dump in the world.

* * *

All farms in Iceland retain their original names, so matching a family history to a good regional map I found Haltbjarnarstaðir, the farm of my great-great-great grandfather—Guðmundur Gudmundsson. I drove to the farmhouse overlooking the ocean. I was concerned because it was a bit late, but I saw a light in the living room, so I knocked on the door. It wasn't long before a middle-aged man appeared.

I explained to him my genealogical tie to that view. He apologized for his shaky English and disappeared into his office, which, like other farm and city homes, was lined floor to ceiling with books. He reappeared with four fossils his daughter had found on the beach below his home. "Here, you should have these . . . they are of this place. You are, too."

* * *

In the car, back by the junkyard, engine off and window open, I finish the last of the coffee in the thermos. The other treasure hunter is now gone. Holding one of the fossils, I look west, out to sea as others have done for centuries. It is satisfying being able to see this far.

Guðmundur Guðmundsson's farm site

Dettifoss, Iceland, 28 June 1993

2:30 AM, stratified cloud cover, cool. I'm tired after a long and rough drive from Mývatn, but I'll sleep along the road after I make a few photographs.

* * *

In *Independent People*, Halldór Laxness's main character, Bjartur of Summerhouses, was flushed down this river after jumping on the back of a frightened bull reindeer in a blizzard. A raging river of glacial icemelt must have been a shock to Bjartur. And a shock it was to Anna's mother when Sigurbjörn made known his plans to leave here with her daughter and granddaughter.

Years before, in 1875, the volcano Askja erupted, devastating the Northeast. It was marginal land to start with, a desert at best, the last settled; then after the blast—volcanic ash and lava everywhere. So, not seeing eye-to-eye with his farming partner, Sigurbjörn decided, like thousands of others, to leave his homeland for good . . . hoping for better.

I don't think Sigurbjörn left in anger. His poetry only mourns the loss of his landscape. But like Bjartur, he was fiercely independent, and he left Iceland with others like him who could make such decisions.

* * *

Sitting outside my tent, the late light and a couple of shots of Laphroaig softens the look of this inhospitable landscape.

Jökulsá á Fjöllum

Mývatn, Iceland, 27 June 1993

Mývatn, which literally means "fly lake," is, without question, well named. 5:00 PM, the light looks clearer to me; after a swim and hot tub there are fewer bugs around me.

* * *

Rosa, Anna's mother, must have been a strong woman. Over a period of years, she and her husband lost three infant daughters. Then her only living daughter, Anna, married Sigurbjörn, bore her own daughter, then one year later their little family walked ninety miles to board a ship for America, leaving Rosa and her husband Guðny behind.

She watched them leave, perhaps in the same way as she watched her three young daughters die. But then two years later, she and Guðny joined them in Mountain late in the fall. Sigurbjörn was working in Winnipeg, so it was their family again—together.

Winter hit. At night during a blizzard, Guðny died. Rosa and her daughter wrapped him in a blanket and laid him in a snowbank. She watched a community struggle to define itself—not an easy task amongst that argumentative lot. She watched other births and deaths and outlived her daughter, Sigurbjörn, and several grandchildren.

* * *

What could she tell us about death . . . about watching?

Mývatn

Barkarstaðir, Iceland, 30 June 1993

2:00 PM, squally, then calm, some rain heading in from the west. I finally found this place, matching a photo of this farmstead my aunt had sent with me. I feel serenity here, as I had hoped, and a quiet power.

* * *

My dad's grandfather, Sæmundur Sigurdson, grew up here and looked at these mountains morning and night. He was a talented man who sewed, cooked, worked in wood, and painted on glass. He was soft-spoken and kindly to others. The photos we have of him show a gentle man.

From his nursing home bed, Jack Thorfinson, a friend of my grandfather, told Bill Holm and me about the time Sæmundur was wallpapering Jack's mother's living room. Jack and his brother were fighting again. After yelling at the boys who were busily bloodying one another, she said in exasperation to Sæmundur, "What am I going to do?" Saying nothing, he went outside, picked up one boy under each arm, walked quietly to the stock tank, and dunked both under the cold water. After a time, he brought them up and said softly, "Listen to your mother." Jack said they did.

* * *

In Wolf Willow, *Wallace Stegner said, "Expose a child to a particular environment at his susceptible time and he will perceive in the shapes of that environment until he dies."*

To what extent does this perception, this bonding, affect one's personality? Back then, without technological distractions, this relationship must have been stronger. The emigrants surely must have carried with them, and been molded by, their native landscapes. So what of Sæmundur, perhaps of me, am I now looking at?

Eyjafjallajökull

West of Höfn, Iceland, 2 July 1993

High noon, clear. It looks hot from inside the air-conditioned car, but I'm guessing it is only about 80 degrees. I'm getting tired from the miles and the lack of sleep.

Fragility and roughness live here together—curious mates. The open road runs like a chalk line snapped on this flat, arid surface.

* * *

In 1856, a zealous group of Mormons convinced a contingent of Icelanders to convert to Mormonism and move to Spanish Fork, Utah. They moved, prospered, and some became Mormons, and very few of them ate cod on a regular basis after that.

Yesterday, winds came up off the North Atlantic, blew my tent down in the middle of the night, and started my day. The rainy winds grew stronger. I took only one shot of a waterfall blowing straight up—vaporized by the gale. Fearful that the wind would shred the bellows on my 4x5 camera, I crawled through the inside of the car, opened the hatch back and, hunkering leeward, made a single exposure.

The Ring Road around Iceland was only completed in the 1970s. Beer was legalized in 1989. Yet, since 874 AD, Icelanders have both traveled widely and drunk enthusiastically. Somehow beer and a section of this road fell between the cracks on the national priority list.

* * *

Now, with the sun well over the yardarm, the thought of a beer on this road makes a great deal of sense.

Ring Road west of Höfn

Keflavik, Iceland, 23 July 1997

As we taxi into takeoff position, I stare out the plane's window in the late afternoon light and the image of rough lava field next to the runway melds with the impressionistic images of the previous long days out on the road.

• • •

A few days ago, I was back in Akureyri, not in search of a poet, not in search of anything, just there walking the streets, without a camera, armed only with knowing it was my ancestral home. I know their names, their farms, and much of their collective history. I know of the connection between those ancestors and specific pieces of geography. Further, I've added my layer, my experiences to this sense of place.

That was where Auðun the Rotten married Helgi the Lean's daughter. They lived along the fjord. It was where their great-grandson Guðmund the Powerful said goodbye to his son, Halldór, as he went off with other Vikings to Ireland—never to see his own son Rafn grow to be a man.

From Auðun, down twenty-three generations to my great-grandfather Sigurbjörn, they lived there in the northeast corner of Iceland in the northeast corner of the Atlantic. What do we know of them, of their daily lives, their thoughts? Nothing really. They kicked around there for roughly 1,000 years, begetting others, being meddlesome, loving, brave, cowardly, and kindly. Doing things poorly and well, but doing so, there.

• • •

The brakes are released and the engine's thrust pushes me back into my seat. So now I leave and head west, back home. But what about east, where did Helgi come from?

West of Nýja Holi, Sigurbjörn Guðmundsson's farm

III. The Search

"There was a man named Grímur Kamban who was the first to settle in the Faroe Islands. In those days, a great number of men were seeking refuge from the tyranny of King Haraldur Fine-Hair; some men settled themselves in the Faroe Islands and farmed there, while other men sought land on other islands."

Opening paragraph in *Faroe-Islander Saga*

The Search

Sigurbjörn Guðmundsson, like so many of his countrymen, wrote poetry and farmed. He was taught to read by an uncle who was a recognized poet. It was in the footnotes of one of his uncle's books that I came across a lineage back twenty-eight generations from me to a man called Grímur Kamban who was the first settler of the Faroe Islands in about 825.

By now, it was clear to me that I was on a hunt that would unfold in the Faroes. I wanted to find my ancestral places and try to learn something about those who lived there. It became a search back against the flow of migration, east instead of west, back into time.

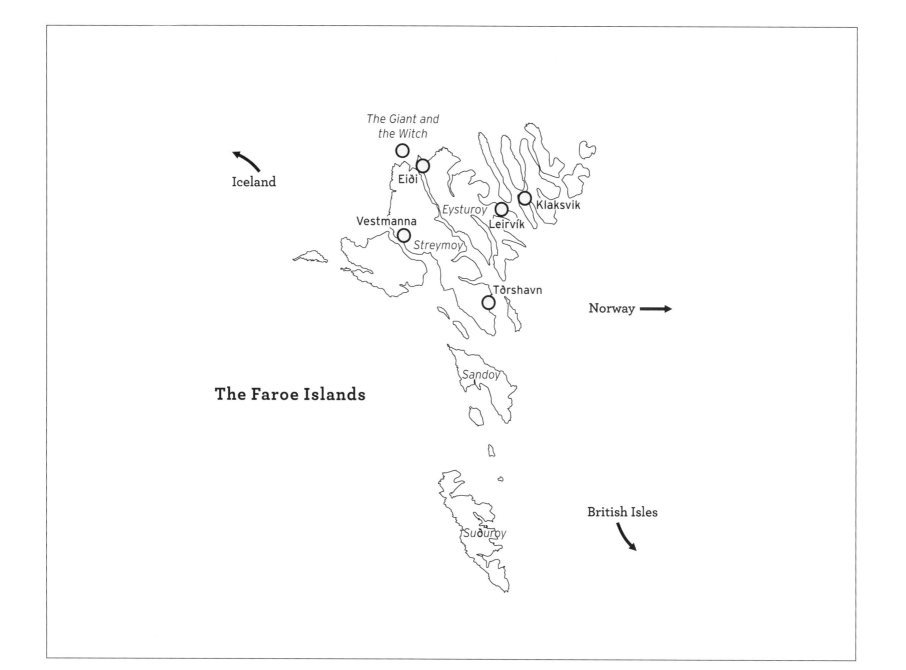

The Giant and the Witch

Iceland

Eiði

Eysturoy

Klaksvík

Vestmanna

Leirvík

Streymoy

Tórshavn

Norway

The Faroe Islands

Sandoy

British Isles

Suðuroy

Tórshavn, Faroe Islands, 15 May 2001

I'm settled in at a guest house facing east out to sea with the old city in a cold evening rain at my back. My search for Grímur Kamban, twenty-eight generations my senior, begins tomorrow.

• • •

"It would seem from this that Irish priests had reached the Faroes soon after the year 700 and lived there undisturbed till the first Norsemen arrived about a hundred years later and dispossessed them. Of these Northmen we know practically nothing, save that the most important among them was Grímur Kamban." (quoted from the *Faroe-Islander Saga*)

"Dispossessing" sounds so sanitized. More likely the dispossessing was done up-close and bloody with no detainees, sometimes, as the sagas state, with a flair and a vengeful joy.

His Celtic surname suggests an arrival from the south, perhaps the Orkneys, Ireland, or most likely the Isle of Man—an early Viking hangout. Everyone and no one seems to know where he lived in the Faroes, but he made a mark here, nonetheless, and entered the written annals. His son, Þorsteinn, bore a son, Þorolfur, who sailed with the Norwegian, Floki Vilgardsson, on his notable early naming trip to Iceland.

It was around this time that the family made their move to Iceland with the marriage of Auðun the Rotten, Þorolfur's son, to Helga, daughter of the regional chieftain, Helgi the Lean—probably just before the year 900. They settled in the north around Eyjafjordur and spent the next 1,000 years meddling about in that region.

• • •

The Icelanders take great stock in the sagas. The Faroese, however, having been given more exposure to the events and effects of the ensuing 1,000 years, hold the sagas to be misty myth at best. It was as if I was in search of Paul Bunyan. "Grímur Kamban," the librarian said. "Well, there is a street by that name in the old town."

Girm Kamban Street, Thorshavn, Faroe Islands

Tórshavn, Faroe Islands, 17 May 2001

10:00 PM, Hotel Hafnia, waiting for my dinner after a long day on the road. I sit in denims in an upscale Faroese restaurant like a carp amongst the silken red salmon and think back to a sea of costumed chain dancers I saw today.

* * *

As I came out of the public library, I saw groups of costumed folks arriving from many directions. They slowly filled the town square, outnumbering the spectators. One person started a song, then they all joined in, singing and moving in unison. Small circles formed, slowly morphing into larger eddies. They flowed tightly, coiling in and around, eventually all interconnecting, repeating the ancient ballads, moving to a national pulse, collectively celebrating something of who they are.

It wasn't until the dance was over and the music stopped that I understood its power. The end was jarring, sending a reverent silence across the packed square. It was as if the perpetual flow of the tides had suddenly stopped. This momentary silence, like an unspoken benediction, blessed the dancers, spoke of their strength, and connected them to an ancient time.

* * *

As I walk through a light mist back across the now empty square, I hear jazz and laughter coming from a corner pub.

West Streymoy

Vestmanna, Faroe Islands, 18 May 2001

In a working man's bar, I watch through cigarette smoke the late afternoon light coming in low over the pool table. It washes over the only other patrons, a rather disparate looking lot, and visually unites them in a soft-focus haze.

∙ ⊚ ∙

Another cheap-beer drinker admitted, "There is a story that I'm from Thrand of Gotu." This is Faroese for saying, "I'm Lee Harvey Oswald's grandson." But still, it's a tie to antiquity—and a Viking connection at that.

Having just read the *Faroe-Islander Saga*, I knew the reference and said, "You have Thrand's red hair, but you appear honest." He laughed heartily and signaled the bartender for another round. The beer got and stayed cheaper.

"My grandmother also tells of a princess who was shipwrecked on Streymoy and became one of us," he said.

∙ ⊚ ∙

To live with such myth, such possibility, connects one to a larger family. The bar is quiet again and after I spread my map out on the pool table the bartender offers his best guess on where to find Grímur's farm.

North Esturoy

Leirvik, Faroe Islands, 19 May 2001

In the car, buffeted by a strong northeasterly wind, I wait. Earlier, I was in the south hoping for a boat trip along the cliffs, which we were told was out of the question because the seas were too high. I headed north to track down the state archaeologist. Now I'm next in line for the ferry to Klaksvik, a soft rain muting the tones and blurring the edges.

* * *

They worked for the second largest paper in Gothenburg, Sweden. He, the photographer, and Peter, the writer, were here to cover the fishing conference and whatever else they could dig up.

He told me of a situation where he took the wrong picture—the event happened in fact, but the photograph didn't represent the truth. We spoke of our dogs, his named Taurus, a collie who recently lost a dog mate. Taurus found a new pal, a lab, but still when allowed to run, returned to the yard of his old friend.

We spoke of the therapy of dog walks, of administration versus being in the field. He said that good pictures crawl toward us like snails and leave like lightning.

As we waited for boarding, I made a portrait with his camera of him and his partner for their paper's upcoming issue. Then after a call from their editor, they pulled out of the line and headed back to Tórshavn to cover an unfolding labor strike. "Farewell my comrade," I said.

* * *

The stern doors of the ferry open like a mouth beginning a slow yawn. I continue on to Klaksvik in search of Grímur Kamban.

Vestmanna

Hotel Eidi, Faroe Islands, 20 May 2001

4:00 PM, strong gusts from the west with alternating hard light and stinging rain. In the best room in the house, empty because of a workers' strike, I comfortably look down the long fjord and back to the pre-Viking times when the Irish monks had mostly free reign, but also knew change from the north was in the wind.

· · ·

"OK, how about . . . there once were two strong . . . fisherman."
Poking the fire with a piece of driftwood, Padraic said, "No, I don't think they'd be interested in such a task. Maybe a giant."
"Yes, perfect, and a feisty librarian," said Shaemus.
"I'm not sure, it's doubtful a librarian would want that kind of labor. What about a giant and his witch of a wife?" said Padriac.
"Or his wife who is a witch," said Shaemus.
Padriac said, "Yes, this is coming together. So the giant Kellin and his wife, Resin the witch, are struck by the beauty of Eidikollur. They throw a rope around it and try to drag it home to Iceland before the next day. After prolonged procedural quarreling, they are caught by the rising sun, turned to stone, and become part of the landscape."
"I think that will do quite nicely, the Norse will love it," said Shaemus. "Ever been to Vinland?"

· · ·

The rain starts to turn to sleet with bits of snow mixed in, softening the rhythm on the window. I'll try to find the owner and scare up a meal, then I'll settle in with The Black Cauldron, *by William Heinesen, which unfolds somewhere through the snow just down the fjord from here.*

The Witch and the Giant

Klaksvik, Faroe Islands, 22 May 2001

After walking the Viking digs with Anna the archeologist, I'm directed here to this picnic ground to look for the many depressions—the future site for future digs, pending funding. That they are Viking-age goes without saying. Which Viking is another question.

. . .

Grímur Kamban most likely lived at Funningur on the north end of Esturoy, and chances are his son Þorsteinn did too. That is probably where Þorolfur left from on his famous trip to Iceland.

The Irish monks visited Iceland early. Gardar Svavarsson, a Swede, made the first recorded run at Iceland, naming it Gardarsholm. Later, Noddod, a Norwegian, paid a visit and dubbed this island Snæland or Snowland. But it was the Norweigen, Floki Vilgerdasson, whose name stuck.

Floki sailed via the Shetlands, where he lost a daughter to drowning, and showed up in the Faroes where he lost another to marriage. Þorolfur, and three recently blessed ravens, joined the crew on their westward journey, probably around 860 AD.

A short way out, Floki turned loose the first raven which flew back to the Faroes. Later, the second was given flight and it circled and then returned to the ship. The third raven was finally released and led the ship to their destination. After a long hungry winter, they returned to Norway. Floki, now going by the name Raven Floki, called the place Iceland. His first mate Herjolf gave the place mixed reviews and Þorolfur, undaunted by ice and lack of hay, reported that butter dripped from every blade of Iceland's grass. For this wildly optimistic testimony he was gratefully, or satirically, nicknamed Þorolfur Smjör or Þorolfur Butter.

. . .

So Grímur Kamban was here, as were others. His remains are here now—somewhere. But his descendants, my ancestors, went west.

Archeological dig site

IV. Place

"I felt their pain, beset by midges,
 Midst the ponds and poplar ridges,
 Here was where they burned their bridges,
 Death's bleak door was held ajar."

Excerpt from *Sandy Bar* by Guttormur S. Guttormsson

Place

Although this family line is long, it is, of course, no more or less significant than any other, except that it is mine. As such, I began to feel an obligation to understand something about it and to make a record of it for my daughter.

I had identified the beginning of the known family continuum in the Faroe Islands. I had evidence of some 1,000 years of life in the northeast corner of Iceland. Now, I needed to follow the family forward in time out onto the vast sea-like landscape in the middle of North America.

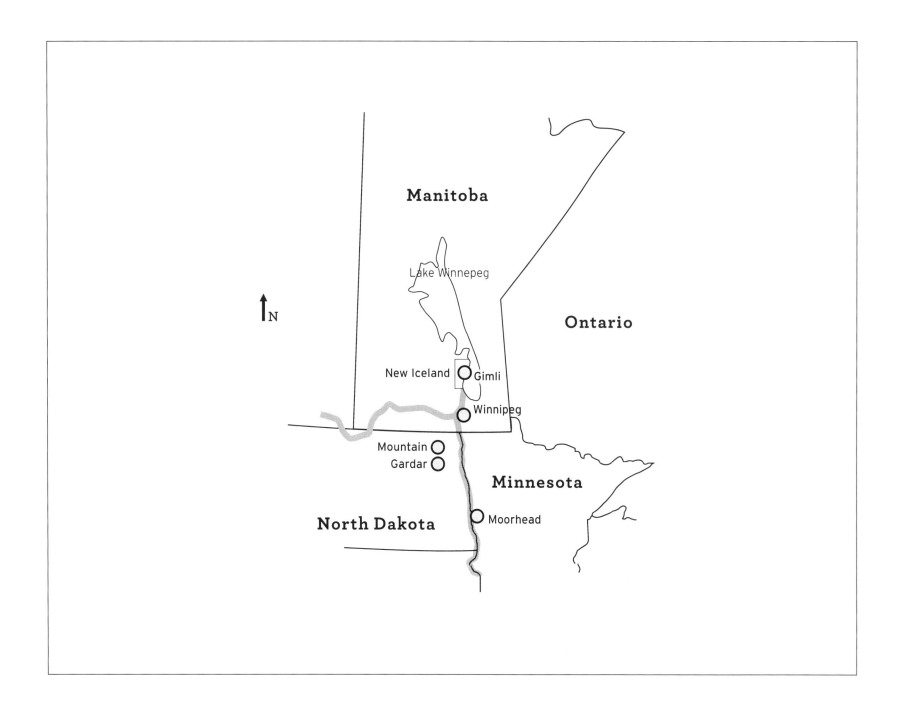

Reykjavík, Iceland, 23 July 1995

The mist rounds the edges of the buildings and boats as I casually explore the old part of town. It's soothing after the extreme weather and topography I experienced this trip around Askja.

* * *

The history of the Icelanders is tied tightly to the sea. During the Viking age they raided, then traded, then settled widely—Novgorod, Kiev, York, Dublin, northern England, Scotland, Ireland, even Normandy. William the Conqueror was the grandson (or was it the great-great-great-grandson) of the Viking chief, Rolf the Ganger. All of this played out because of their prowess on the sea, but early on, I realized that it was their land and their literature that they loved most—they had little else.

In 1856, Lord Dufferin, then a young man, visited Iceland. In *Letters from a High Latitude*, he spoke of his fascination for this magic place and literate people. Dufferin went on to become the Viceroy of India; then he landed the position of Governor General of Canada. In 1875 Askja erupted, sending ash over the northeast corner, ruining the overcrowded, marginal grazing land. Dufferin was approached by a group of Icelanders with a plan—help us set up a republic in Canada. In 1875, New Iceland, approximately 5x35 miles on the west coast of Lake Winnipeg, came to be. It was there, they hoped, that they could keep their language and ethnicity intact. With this simultaneous push and pull, many left Iceland.

First they traveled to Edinburgh; then Glasglow; then Montreal; Duluth and Moorhead, Minnesota; and on up to Fort Garry (Winnipeg); then finally north to New Iceland. They left Iceland on boats like the Camoens that took Sigurbjörn and his little family.

* * *

The mist has given way to fog. It's good to walk these streets. Soon I'll have to board a plane for Minneapolis. A lone gray granite figure stands at the end of the walking street. It's hard to tell who it is. I heard that there's a statue somewhere in Reykjavík dedicated to the lone Icelander who doesn't write.

Askja Crater Lake

Gimli, Manitoba, 2 August 1991

The light is strong without being too hard, and we're cooled by a faint welcome wind. It is a good day to make pictures in this calm before the storm. Bill drives and David Arnason directs us back to his cabin on Willow Point. We've come in waves from all directions, like Norse invaders, to robustly celebrate our heritage.

* * *

Earlier in the day we visited Sandy Bar, the site Guttormur Guttormsson made famous in his epic ballad of Icelandic settlement. There we found one lone fisherman, an old man of Ukrainian descent putting his gear into the back of his old half-ton pickup. David was talking with him, I was making a photo, and Bill was rustling around in the car. He returned with a copy of Guttormur's poem, which he read to the three of us with the passion that the work deserved. "Once a walk at midnight taking, Gusts of rain around me shaking, Sky and earth alight and quaking . . ." Poetry lived there for a moment.

Bill and David discussed, argued, and alternately held forth on a variety of topics from post-modernism to politics to recipes for Icelandic desserts. These were not men of weak opinion. Nor were the Reverends Jon Bjarnasson and Pall Thorlaksson. Strong differences on desserts can be tolerated, but not religion. Jon and his band stayed in Gimli in 1878 when Pall took his followers south across some of the best farmland in North America until they came to the rise on the west edge of the Red River Valley and, like puffins, settled there amongst the rocks.

* * *

This morning, Bill and I waded through the carnage of last night's partying and with relief not only found our car, but found it intact. Few could be accused of moderation last night. After picking up a newspaper and a couple of coffees, we drive south. Bill carefully adjusts his newly bandaged leg—a casualty from the previous night—opens the paper, and says, "Jesus Christ, Saddam Hussein has invaded Kuwait."

Sandy Bar, Lake Winnipeg

Thingvalla Church cemetery, North Dakota, 16 October 2003

A brisk wind out of the northwest, 28 degrees, the low midday sun fully illuminates K.N.'s monument now that the church is gone. There to the right, and back a couple of rows, lie a sizeable group of Guðmundson markers clustered around Sigurbjörn's stone.

· · ·

Sigurbjörn only spent a year or so in Gimli before homesteading about a mile and a half from here in 1881 at a farm they named Brautarholt. With Anna, they raised their family. He was active in the community and at this church. In fact, he was quite active.

By June of 1910, when Sigubjörn was fifty years old, a difference of opinion had made its way onto paper and polarized the community. The correspondence was first only within the church, but by October it had entered the legal system. Sigurbjörn and a minority of the church membership sued the majority for the "possession of the premises" and "use of the property," as they had sacked a minister because of his literal interpretation of the scriptures. The divisive proceedings weren't settled in the lower court until February of 1912—three months after his wife, Anna, had died.

Sigurbjörn's health declined so that in May 1914 he went to Winnipeg for an operation and died of heart failure during the procedure. He was buried in his cemetery next to Anna and one of their children. Six months later, the North Dakota Supreme Court overturned the decision and the remaining plaintiffs had to cough up over $1,200 and give back the use of the church to the majority of the congregation.

A couple of months ago, I was talking to the grandson of one of the defendants in that case about the day the church burned down. As they watched the brittle building consume itself, he told a neighbor that he was glad their grandfathers didn't have to see this happen.

· · ·

K.N.'s monument now dwarfs all of the other man-made structures here at this old battleground.

Sigurbjörn Guðmundsson and Anna Guðnadöttir's farm site

Mountain, North Dakota, 6 August 1980

10:30 PM, a soft warm night, no moon affords us a view of all the stars that ever were. We gather to conduct business, to bury Grandpa Chris, to stay one last time as a family in his house—here at the one full intersection in Mountain.

* * *

Fresh out of the navy, I took a job driving a dirt truck and was told to take an old, battered, mostly yellow Kenworth up to Langdon, North Dakota and be at work at six the next day. Needing a room for the night, a buddy and I pulled our rigs up next to the Mountain Cash store, across from Grandpa Chris's, and went in search of him. His Ford was gone, which it usually was, so we found a stool at Byron's Bar, kitty-corner from Chris's.

At about 11:00 PM, Chris strolled into the bar, shaking hands and greeting every person, working the crowd like a seasoned politician. When he came to the two long-hairs at the end of the bar, his initial look of displeasure switched to joy when he realized the place held one more Gudmundson. "Three beers," he said to Duwayne Byron. "A game of pool, boys?"

As a young man, Chris had run a pool hall in Winnipeg. "Sixteen tables, I played every day. I was good." He said, "Well, what will it be, Last Pocket, Once on the Eight, Nine Ball, Slop?" I too, had grown up playing pool, and eventually came to appreciate and sometimes play with the old-style finesse. It was Ball in Pocket, Once on the Eight. Our game was replete with push shots, cross-corners, kick shots, devilish safe shots and ample verbal jibes—pool as it should be played. In the end, only the eight-ball remained on the table, and I had a shot to win. It wasn't that my competitiveness dictated a win, but it was a matter of good form that required me to make it. To miss a simple once-back would have diminished the game. It would have been disrespectful. I shot it with the reverence that the moment deserved. Ball in, game done. I was drained, exhilarated, and sad. Although the game we played that night has lasted for years, it, like life, was over too soon. Chris bought another round. We closed the bar and walked through that warm August night back to his house. I slept for a few hours on the porch under my favorite print of a seaside village.

* * *

Tonight, the light over the pool table at Byron's is off.

Chris and Stina Gudmundson's

Mountain, North Dakota, 14 March 1995

38 degrees, barely any wind, the light is so flat it denies texture and any sense of depth. I drive through the slushy rain to Bill's Bar, not Byron's today. The pool table is gone. Cheap sacramental wine offers itself on the right and a few bar basics sit confidently, but alone, on the left. "Some bourbon in a glass," I say to Bill's wife. "Did you know old K.N.?" I ask. "No, I didn't move here until '46," she says.

* * *

There was a similar light on the third floor of the Cavalier Hospital where Arni Johnson was dying.

The lone nurse on that floor pointed me to his room. He looked smaller than before and very alone. The only sound was the soft rattle coming from his throat. I touched his forehead and said loudly, "Arni, this is Wayne, Chris Gudmundson's grandson." He opened his watery eyes, the old twinkle gone. I wiped mine. A wisp of recognition appeared, and he tried to say something that I couldn't understand. I touched his forehead again. He closed his eyes and the rattle returned. I looked out the window, through the light rain, southwest towards Mountain.

Arni, you were a friend to me, my father, and my grandfather. In a typical Icelandic fashion, you and Chris sparred over everything. You drove Fords to his Chevys; you a democrat, he a republican; Chris a Lutheran, you a freethinker.

Tell me more about the old days in Mountain. Your wry wit and keen insights always opened new perspectives. Yet, like today, you kept something from me.

I had asked why there are two churches in Gardar within sight of one another, why the rift in the community, why my grandparents weren't buried with their parents. Why didn't you tell me that it was my great-grandfather Sigurbjörn that sued the church on God's behalf? I later found the case—Gudmundson et al vs. the Thingvalla Lutheran Church. Will they bury you at Thingvalla, Vikur, or Vidalin? No, none of that seems right. Besides you weren't meant to die. But then, neither was Mountain. You never went to funerals. I won't go to yours. Rest now, Arni Johnson.

* * *

The old, mangy dog finally moves, allowing me to do a sweeping U-turn and head back—left at the Dead End sign, past the old folks home, right onto ND #32, past Arni's place and south to Moorhead.

Bill's Bar

Bad Medicine Lake, Minnesota, 4 July 1998

Accommodating breeze, clear and sunny—a perfect day to celebrate our anniversary and to belatedly observe Dad's birthday by watching him stand on his head. Last week, while going over a curb, he'd fallen off his bike because the carpentry tools he was carrying on his handlebars threw off his balance. He'd bruised his ribs. The bike and tools were OK, he'd said.

• • •

About ten years ago, I watched Dad ride around the yard backwards on his bike while sitting on the handlebars. He also twirled rope, and as a kid did back flips off fences. Like many of the other kids in Mountain, he enjoyed the poetry of K.N. Once K.N. even inscribed a copy of his book for the young Arinbjorn—later renamed Ed.

For some reason, the reciting of poetry always took place at Arni's. One of the earliest poems of K.N.'s that I remember Dad reciting went like this:

Kom til Gardar, kilneg fret	Come to Gardar, timely news
A K.N. vaeir dian	that K.N. was dead.
Pa var petta ekk jett	Though it was not right
Par var bera pafinn	It was just the Pope.

This always brought laughter. Another K.N. poem was about the annual "August the Deuce" in Mountain.

Many left in drunken sail,	Women served their coffee swill,
Everywhere flows beer and ale,	Men ranted speeches at their will,
Whiskey? No one lacked a bit,	There was singing and there was dance,
Cause Swain and Dor were selling it.	And there was I and Reverend Hans.

Again, knee-slapping laughter. I asked Arni why this was so funny. Arni said that Reverend Hans Thorgrímsen wasn't there and was very much against drinking.

• • •

Now with drinks in hand, we gather on a flat spot behind our cabin. There always seems to be things that we pleasantly cannot understand—like why Dad chose to start standing on his head. Now for some reason, Dad is pinning a piece of paper on his shirt. It appears to be the number 18. "Cameras ready," he says. Up he goes, and one minor mystery is solved. Happy 81st Birthday, Dad!

Gardar, North Dakota

V. Song

"O'er Mithgarth Hugin and Munin both
Each day set forth to fly;
For Hugin I fear lest he come not home,
But for Munin my care is more."

Grímnismál, from *The Poetic Edda*

In Norse mythology, Odin is seen as the primary god and is associated with wisdom, battle, death, healing, language, and poetry. He is often depicted with two ravens—Hugin (old Norse for "thought") and Munin (Old Norse for "memory")—who as messengers fly off over the world, Midgard, each day and return to the shoulders of Odin in the evening to share their findings.

Song

In the early Viking era, Norwegians moved west—many eventually settling in Iceland. In the late 1800s, large contingents not only from Iceland, but from across many northern European countries moved to America and settled in little pockets amongst their own folk. World politics and the economy dictated a further diffusion of these cultural enclaves. From Mountain, North Dakota, many moved west to Seattle, and others south to Grand Forks and Fargo, and—as was the case in my family—to Moorhead.

This movement seemed regular. Life progresses in a mostly predictable fashion, that is, until you have a child. Then all of the boring clichés become profound, mysterious, and wonderfully true.

The record of my search for ancestral landscapes now passed me in time and started to include my daughter's imprint, her travels, and her places.

Moorhead, Minnesota, 23 November 2003

The first blizzard of the season is at work outside, while I'm at work in the darkroom printing the "Wheelock" image and thinking of a family of grain elevators. Upstairs, in the office next to the cancelled checks are your ashes. We could never scatter them; never even considered it.

● ● ●

In 1980, somewhere along the inland passage of Alaska—I think it was in Wrangle or maybe Petersburg—we decided to try for a family. It was an amazing feeling.

This was also the trip where I learned that my photos could be funny. From that three-month trip, I brought back more than one hundred rolls of film that I seriously under-agitated in development, rendering them almost unprintable. I was sick to my stomach.

Later that fall I met with Mrs. Korsmo, my fifth-grade teacher. It was in her class that I finally learned to read. My reading level went from second to tenth grade. She was married to the undertaker, and it was she who handed me your ashes on another very cold day. I was surprised how heavy they were.

● ● ●

Your brief time with us has informed and affected us in ways we could never imagine—not a small gift, my stillborn son.

Wheelock, North Dakota

Hotel Sofitel, Minneapolis, 21 November 2003

In the spacious lobby, we eat escargot and sea scallops, and drink wine in celebration of the art opening of one of your godmothers. Liv, Patrice is your Mom's soul mate to be sure, and our surprise attendance brought joy to them both.

* * *

The order of events has started to become meaningless. The whole is seldom defined by one act, but is more tempered by many. Still, certain images are as if they are currently unfolding.

I had always made fun of dads showing pictures of their new babies. Getting to the liquor store five minutes late the night after you were born, I found the door locked and the employees closing up. I pressed a small sampling of my collection of baby pictures to the glass door and pounded away until they took notice. The manager came over and reluctantly opened up. I barged in and shamelessly laid out a formidable one-day retrospective of your life. Other employees gathered to look at the pictures. I bought beer and wine, and with cheers and laughter they gave me a bottle of champagne on my way out.

* * *

Looking at the French impressionistic mural behind the reception desk as I check in, I think of you, Liv, in Mulhouse, France. We've all traveled many miles in the last sixteen years. It's four in the morning there, and here I'm warmed with wine and the image of you and your traveling buddy, "Mouse," curled up, asleep in mid-adventure.

Mississippi River Headwaters

Somewhere North of Langdon, North Dakota, 4 January 1985

Heavy snow, wind must be at least 30 miles an hour, temperature can't be more than 10 degrees. A line of trees looks promising. Light meter, camera, tripod, film packs, dark-cloth ready. The technical preparation is as routine as opening the thermos and pouring coffee. It's a dance I've done a thousand times. In making pictures, photographers, outside of technical stuff, really only have three variables—place, time, and vantage point.

* * *

The place was Liv's first grade classroom at Riverside Elementary in Moorhead, and the time was thirty-eight years after I sat in the very same room as a first grader. Liv's desk was even in the same place—facing north on the window side of the room. I was on my way to a parents-day event and was fully prepared to be flooded with memories and emotions, but I stood there cold and confused, disappointed that I felt nothing.

Liv wanted to show me how she'd arranged the inside of her desk. I got down on my knees, at her eye-level, and looked in at her desk. As I looked up and around at her environment, it happened instantly. There was the latticework on the air vent, the gray window handle, the exact angle of the tiles as they met the bookcase molding. That precise vantage point reconnected me with that time and to those old visual mantras for my daydreaming.

* * *

Back in the car, the coffee warms and helps me regroup a bit. I had walked into the field, found the right spot, and was moving around the camera and tripod, preparing to make an exposure when it happened—a total whiteout. It became hard to breathe because of the intensity of the blowing snow. My first instinct was to head toward the car, but I had lost all sense of direction. I stood there for what seemed a very long time before the trees appeared as if in a dream. I made two exposures and beat it out of there. Now another whiteout, and in the safety of the car, I take another sip of coffee and think about what it means to find the right vantage point.

White out west of Mountain

Darkroom, Moorhead, Minnesota, 12 September 1995

Soft yellow from the safelight, classical music, good coffee, and bad negatives. Guðmundur's generous offer to help machine-develop my sheet film to avoid the X-ray machines made all of the 500 negatives very contrasty. Now, I look at these images with their whites, too white to conventionally print. Still this trip was a success.

• • •

The very first trip was quite by accident. I was on my way, via Luxembourg, to Copenhagen to do my student teaching. As I checked in at the ticket counter of Icelandair in New York, one young agent looked at my passport and said, "Oh, you're Icelandic. You're going to Iceland." "No, I'm going to Luxembourg," I said. "You're Icelandic. You're going to Iceland." I thought that there was a language problem and that it was his.

His partner came over to see what was going on as he repeated it again, this time more slowly. Both men nodded. It then dawned on me that it was I who misunderstood. "OK," I said.

They changed my ticket, gave me three nights free lodging in Reykjavík and a voucher for meals.

Even then as a twenty-four-year-old, I began to understand there was an unspoken national kinship. It wasn't until much later that I learned the rest of the axiom. There are three things Icelanders hold most dearly—their language, their landscape, and themselves.

• • •

These negatives will be hard to print. It is more than just over-development, it's the light. The rarified light of Iceland—so clear, so unfouled—is more than I can comfortably handle.

South of Seyðisfjörður

North Atlantic, 4 August 1998

Onboard Icelandair Flight 223—two years since my last entry in this diary. My first trips to Iceland were to explore and research, to make pictures, to respond to that landscape and to my ethnicity. I return with Jane and Liv, not to take images away, but to give back my impressions in the form of a book and an exhibit.

* * *

I wonder what the Icelanders will think of what I saw of their home. Was I too harsh, too patronizing? Will they appreciate the terse humor? I'm not sure, although I do know that they won't withhold their opinions . . . but I'm more curious to learn what Liv and Jane will make of this hauntingly strange place.

Liv said that she wants to see some puffins, ride an Icelandic horse, and get into as many hot springs as possible. I expect she will, but what will she see through her little camera? What will she capture in her pictures? My hope is that at some later point she'll find something of herself waiting patiently there in the film's emulsion.

* * *

With her nose pressed to the plane's window, she watches as the Wagnerian sky slowly slides from a convincing black to a mid-tone gray as we descend in the early morning light towards Keflavik.

Liv asks, yet again, "How much longer, Dad?" "The plane should land soon," I say as I hand her some film for her camera. Here, load up, my tourist-class Valkyrie. Scour the battlefields, gather the bravest and the best.

South of Vopnafjörður

Westman Island, Iceland, 16 August 1998

Sky clear, wind 2–5 knots NNW. The warm sun and gentle rocking put me to sleep on the ferry back to Þorlákshöfn on the main island.

* * *

From a lawn chair with beer and binoculars in hand, I watched Liv and Jane scale the 300-foot extinct crater wall surrounding our campsite. After their descent, the three of us exchanged our varied perceptions on the height and difficulty of the climb.

Every August, the adult puffins give the webbed boot to their young to head out to sea, to live, to fish, to mature. For the past several hundred years many of these puffin pilgrims have gotten distracted by the lights of Heimay and ended up stranded in the city streets. The local children, armed with flashlights and boxes, rescue these wayfarers between midnight and three, and then release them the next morning.

That night, Liv joined forces with a new campground friend—one Tryggvi Stefanson. Liv and Tryggvi and a parental escort headed into the city near midnight. I was awakened at 2:00 AM and found myself nose to beak with an equally shocked and disgusted young puffin. After breaking camp the next morning, we headed in a caravan to the beach. The release was a joyous, exciting, and sad occasion filled with a curious hope and sense of purpose. The two hunters were, I think, surprised by the poignancy of the moment.

* * *

So today one small puffin heads out to sea.

Tryggvi and Liv

VI. THE CIRCLE

In the twelfth century, Icelander Snorri Sturlasson wrote the Sagas of the Norwegian Kings. This collection became known as the *Heimskringla*. This name was derived from the first two words of one of the manuscripts— "kringla heims," meaning "circle of the world."

In Viking times, myth and fact sailed the seas together.

The Vegvísir, also known as the runic compass or the Viking compass, made of eight Viking rune staves, is a symbol of protection and guidance. If worn or displayed on a ship, one would never lose their way in storms or bad weather even when the way is not known.

The Circle

In my search, it was becoming evident that the family saga or songline would occasionally circle back and over itself. This occurred often in Iceland, but also in Edinburgh, Scotland; and on the Isle of Man, which sits strategically between England and Ireland.

Port Erin, Isle of Man, 25 July 2007

From a used bookstore I watch the accommodating light move across the old seaside hotels that face the harbor. They sprang up in the 1880s after Queen Victoria gave her royal blessing to this holiday spot in the Irish Sea. However, this island's resort status was not new.

• • •

Long before the monasteries at Lindesfarn and Iona were sacked in the mid-to-late 800s signaling the start of the Viking Age, the Norse had found this place, and found it to be comfortable. Grímur was one of those, but he didn't stay. The Faroe-Islander Saga says that Grímur picked up the Celtic name Kamban here. No doubt a gift from a local woman, soon to be mother to many generations to follow.

But why leave? Was it the pull—the promise of new land—that drove them north? Did Odin, like the Lutheran God to follow, not favor such comfort? More likely it was the allure of the openness and opportunity of the sea that pulled them away and onward. Their sons born in the Faroes did the same as young men, as they continued west to Iceland.

How curious that seven generations later another Guðmundson, Halldór by name, should travel back through here on his way to an event that would mark both his end and that of the Viking era.

• • •

Earlier this morning, Liv suggested we all explore alone and meet for lunch. At last, I see her round the corner and head my direction, saving me from my feeble attempt to get into The Manxman *by Hall Cain. In each country I travel to, I try to find a writer to help me get a sense of the place. This book will remain on the island.*

Looking southwest to the Irish Sea

Port Erin, Isle of Man, 26 July 2007

With the tide out, the small boats rest on the long, sandy beach teased by the light 10 knot breeze off the sea. As I walk along hunting for shells, I'm warmed by the mid-day sun and the knowledge that I'm here.

. . .

Halldór, we come through time, to say goodbye, to wish you well on this, your last voyage. Tomorrow you'll die on the beaches of Ireland.

The word must have gone out months before calling in the longboats brimming with testosterone—arriving from the Orkneys, Shetlands, Faroes, the Hebrides, and from the Viking hangouts across Iceland, England, and Scandinavia.

They met on the Isle of Man and en masse set sail, arriving just offshore, north of Dublin. Then, as the sun was setting, they sailed back east as if in retreat until they were out of sight. Hoping to catch the Irish off guard on a Holy Day, they returned at sunrise and came ashore with swords drawn.

It was a gamble for land, for spoils, and for the bragging rights in the mead halls of the North. Opposite them were bands of Irish and other Norsemen lead by the senior Irish chieftain Brian Boru.

The ensuing carnage would not be new. Rather, it was a primal dance, performed too often, beyond logic, fueled by a virulent male gene. This gene, unlike the men, would survive until such time that the weapons themselves would one day inherit it.

. . .

The tide is now in, and the uninitiated eagerly shove off with laughter to try their young hands at sailing.

The fleet at rest

Dublin, Ireland, 28 May 2003

Wednesday, no wind to speak of. These peaceful, prosperous oaks, descendants of those that on that Good Friday in 1014 "dripped red with blood," now shade the BMWs and the occasional Bentley in the parking lot around the Clontarf Castle Hotel—the site where Brian Boru was killed.

* * *

Boru was the Irish king whose collected forces, including mercenary Vikings, defeated the Norse Vikings. That battle, according to many medieval historians, marked the end of the Viking era. Boru, his sons, and most of the warring leaders died that day.

Halldór Guðmundsson, son of Guðmund the Powerful, also fell that day. Did he die in the oaks alongside his comrade, Asmund the White, or on the only bridge back to the Viking city Dublin while Styggir and his meddlesome mother watched from the safety of the castle? Or was he cut down on the mucky shore during the late afternoon high tide that prevented their retreat back to the ships? It's impossible to say—except that he did—adding his life, his death, to the 10,000 plus that fouled the field and shore on that holy day.

At the end of the battle, with the outcome certain and the Irish closing in, a retreating Viking named Thorstein knelt to tie his boot. When asked why he stopped, he said, "Because I can't make it to my Icelandic home tonight." Whether it was the surprising candor or the fact that there had been enough killing, he was spared and later returned home. Others stayed.

* * *

Now, the light is a bit flat and the street noise tiring as I head into the Brian Boru Pub near Clontarf. While the corned beef is being cut to join the cabbage and the new potatoes on my plate, the server asks about my accent, "Are we American today?" "Yes, and I was yesterday," I say. We share smiles, then she asks, "And tomorrow?"

The Battleground

Joppa, Scotland, 3 August 2007

The Firth of Forth just east of Edinburgh, the wind is fresh from the north and the light is sharp. We're here for the wedding of Johnnie and Fiona, who is the daughter of Jane's old friends Neil and Eileen. They're godparents to Liv, and we to their first daughter.

* * *

Before being put into service hauling loads of emigrants from Iceland, the small cargo ship named the Camoens transported scores of free-roaming Icelandic ponies who were bound for the coal mines of the midlands of England and Wales where they lived underground, never seeing the light of day again or feeling the wind in their faces.

It was past here in 1882 that Sigurbjörn, Anna, and their one-year-old daughter sailed in from Iceland on the same ship and docked just up the firth at Leith. From there they took a train to Glasgow to pick up a ship for the New World.

At what point do people stop being emigrants and become immigrants? Is there a mid-point in the Atlantic where they are notified of the change in their collective status? I expect they remain emigrants until they die, and perhaps only later do their children begin to think of themselves as immigrants.

Regardless, their stay in Scotland was brief and fleeting, like shadows passing on the sand.

* * *

Now a border collie appears and greets us with her treasure. She only drops it to bark at a departing ship.

The Firth of Forth

Dalsfjord, Norway, 9 August 2007

The north side of the fjord, just off the ferry from Dale. I'm sitting with coffee in hand at the base of the statue of Ingólfur Arnarson. The sun has sneaked out, but it looks like rain may be closing in, maybe only fog.

* * *

So I found it at long last—sort of. It was here in 874 that Arnarson left Norway to sail with his followers to settle Iceland. They had grown weary of the heavy-handed politics of the emerging power of Harold Fairhair. No doubt there were other and varied reasons for this move. But they were united by the simple and difficult act of leaving, leaving their homeland.

In *Growth of the Soil*, Knut Hamsun wrote about those Norwegians who were "of the land," and his countryman Johan Boyer in *The Last of the Vikings* told of those who were "of the sea." At this point, who really knows where Grímur Kamban came from in Norway? The scholars only say that he hailed from somewhere along the southwest coast. I'm somewhere along the southwest coast. So that's as close as I'll get. Yet I do know that both Grímur Kamban and Ingólfur Arnarson were men of the sea.

* * *

I pour the cold coffee out and realize that my search is over. I'm not sure what it was that I found—perhaps only the sweet, misty taste of time.

Approaching Dalsfjord

AFTERWORD

Some twenty-five years ago, this work—like so many—started without my knowing it.

While photographing in Iceland, I began to see glimpses or snapshots of fragments of my family history set in that country. At that time our daughter, whom we named Liv—which means Life—was only six years old.

As a new parent, I was awed by the idea of life, and hers in particular. I wanted to share that feeling of place and places as they fit into the larger fabric of a continuum of lives lived.

More recently the next generation has appeared in the energetic form of her son and the arrival of her daughter. So now my hope is that her "Song" will have another verse and be sung by her children.

Wayne Gudmundson
Bad Medicine Lake, Minnesota
2021

Acknowledgments

I thank Bill Holm, with whom I shared many hours and miles talking of the life and work of K.N. Július. Because of our work-in-progress, I made my first photo shoot to Iceland, and without realizing it, began this project. Along the Icelandic roads I read Halldór Laxness and a most respectable family history written by Andrea Jonason, a Canadian of Scottish descent. It was from this fortuitous gift of information that I was able to begin to explore my ancestral landscapes.

While in Iceland, I had the good pleasure of being befriended by Guðmundur Ingolfsson and Halla Hauksdottir. For their consistent and generous hospitality, thank you.

In Gimli, I found inspiration, accommodation, and friendship at the David Arnason compound on Willow Point. I thank Kenneth Smemo for his enthusiastic scholarship of all things Scandinavian, and Sigrid Johnson from the DeFoe Library at the University of Manitoba who helped translate and decode the phrase, "The Battle of Clontarf."

I thank my two press agents—my aunts Rose Gudmundson and May Hermann for their good cheer, energy, and support.

Early on, Angela Glaser kindly helped me with my tortured copy. And, at just the right moment, Doug Carlson appeared to significantly help shape the entire manuscript. I feel fortunate to have had his wise counsel, kindly assistance, and friendship.

To simply say thank you to my wife, Jane, for all that she's given to me and so many others does not seem quite enough. It is because of her, I have been able to do my work.

Anyone who has traveled understands that it is the folks along the road that make the journey. To them and all of the above kind souls, please accept my sincere thanks.

Appendix
A branch of the family tree of Grímur Kamban

Grímur Kamban, first settler of the Faroe Islands
Þorsteinn (Skrofa) Grímmsson
Þorolfur (Smjör) Þorsteinsson—early explorer of Iceland, naming it land of dripping butter
Auðun (the Rotin) Þorolfsson
Einar Auðunsson
Eyulfur Einarsson
Guðmundur (the Powerful) Eyulfsson
Halldór Guðmundsson—died in Battle of Clontarf 1014
Rafn Halldórsson
Eyulfur Rafnsson
Grímur Eyulfsson
Jon Grímsson
Skuli Johnsson
Hakon Skúlasson
Skúli Hakonársson
Bjarni Skúlasson
Hrólfur (the strong) Bjarnasson
Sigurdur Hrolfsson
Hrólfur Sigurdsson
Arngrímur Hrólfsson
Páll Arngrímsson
Guðmundur Guðmundsson and Ingunn Pálsdóttir
Guðmundur Guðmundsson
Svien Guðmundsson
Guðmundur Svienbjörnsson 1821–1868 and Arnbjörns Arnadottir 1827–1876
Sigurbjörn Guðmundsson 1855–1914 and Anna Guðnadottir 1855–1911
Chris Gudmundson 1891–1980 and Stina Sigurdson 1889–1970
Edward Arinbjörn Gudmundson 1917–2017 and Opal Lebakken 1918–2010
Wayne Marvin Gudmundson 1949 and Jane Ann Edwards 1946
Liv Edwards Gudmundson 1987 and Raphaël Devreker 1982
Emile Gudmundson 2015 and Colette Gudmundson 2019

Notes

1. AN INTRODUCTION

Kvidlingar Og Kvaedi, Kristján N. Julíus (K.N.), Bokfellsutgafan H.F., Reykjavik, Iceland, 1945

The Songlines, Bruce Chatwin, Penguin Books, New York, 1987

The Dead Get by With Everything, Bill Holm, Milkweed Editions, Minneapolis, 1990

Nyja Island: Saga of the Journey to New Iceland, Gudjon Arngrimsson, Turnstone Press, Winnipeg, Canada, 1997

The Jonassons: A Family History, Andrea Jonasson, Calgary, Manitoba, 1984

Vesturfaraskra, A Record of Emigrants from Iceland to America, 1870-1914, Junius H. Kristinsson, Institute of History, University of Iceland, Reykjavik, 1983

2. THE LAND

Independent People, Halldor Laxness, Alfred A. Knopf, New York, 1946

Wolf Willow, Wallace Stegner, University of Nebraska Press, Lincoln, 1962

Paradise Reclaimed, Halldor Laxness, Thomas Y. Crowell Company, New York, 1962

3. THE SEARCH

From the Vikings to the Reformation: A Chronicle of the Faeroe Islands up to 1538, G.V.C.Young, Shearwater Press, Douglas, Isle of Man, 1979

The Faeroe Islanders' Saga, translated by George Johnston, Oberon Press, 1975

The Faroe-Islander Saga, translated by Robert K. Painter,McFarland & Company 2016

The Black Cauldron, William Heinesen, Dedalus Ltd. England, 1949

A History of the Vikings, Gwyn Jones, Oxford University Press, London, England,1973

Njal's Saga, translated by Magnus Magnusson and Hermann Palsson, Penguin, London, 1960

Landnamabok, The Book of Settlements, translated by Hermann Palsson and Paul Edwards, University of Manitoba Press, 1972

4. PLACE

"Sandy Bar" by Guttormur S. Guttormsson, *The Icelanders*, ed D. Arnason and M. Olito, Winnipeg Turnstone Press, 1988

Letters from High Lattitudes, Lord Dufferin, J.M.Dent, London, 1910

Framfari: 1877-1880, Gimli Chapter, Icelandic National League of North America, Winnipeg, Canada 1986

Icelandic Settlers in America, Elva Simundsson, Queenston House Publishing, Winnipeg, Manitoba, 1981

Modern Sagas: The Story of the Icelanders in North America, Thorstina Walters, North Dakota Institute for Regional Studies, Fargo, North Dakota, 1953

The Icelandic People in Manitoba, R.W.Kristjanson, Winnipeg, Manitoba, 1965

North Dakota Supreme Court records

Kvidlingar Og Kvaedi, Kristján N. Július (K.N.), Bokfellsutgafan H.F., Reykjavik, Iceland, 1945

5. THE SONG

Grimnimál, The Poetic Edda, Oxford World's Classics, translated by Carolyn Larrington, 2014

6. THE CIRCLE

Heimskringla, History of the Kings of Norway by Snorri Sturlasson, University of Texas Press, Seventh printing 2009

The Galdrabók, an Icelandic Book of Magic, Stephen E. Flowers, Lodestar, 2011

Manxman, Hall Caine, Second Edition, Appleton and Company 1894

Vesturfaraskra, A Record of Emigrants from Iceland to America, 1870-1914, Junius H. Kristinsson, Institute of History, University of Iceland, Reykjavik, 1983

The Growth of the Soil, Knut Hamson, translated by Sverre Lyngstad, Penguin Classics, 2011

The Last Viking, Johan Bojer, New American Library, 1964

In addition to specific references listed by section, I have drawn material from the following sources:

A World Lit Only by Fire, William Manchester, Little, Brown and Company, 1993

Iceland from Past to Present, Esbjorn Rosenblad and Rakel Sigurdardottir-Rosenblad, Mal og Menning, Reykjavik, 1993

Iceland: The Dire Years, Frank Ponzi, Brennholt, Mosfellsbair, Icleand, 1995

Last Places: A Journey in the North, Lawrence Millman, Houghton Mifflin, Boston, 1990

Laxdaela Saga, Penguin Books, Harmondsworth, England, 1969

Letter from Iceland, W.H.Auden and Louiis Macneice, Random House, New York 1937

Norse Gods and Heroes, Morgan K. Roberts, Michael Friedman Puublishing Group, New York, 1995

Ring of Seasons: Iceland – Its Culture, History, Terry G. Lacy, University of Michigan Press, Ann Arbor, 1998

The Complete Sagas of Icelanders, General Editor Vidar Hreinsson, Leifur Eiriksson Publishing, Reykjavik, 1997

The Laxdaela Saga, Translated by Muriel Press, Forgotten Books, 2008

The Norse Myths, Kevin Crossley-Holland, Pantheon Books, New York, 1980

The Prose Edda, Snorri Sturluson, translated by Rasmus B. Anderson, Digireads, 2017

The Sagas Of Icelanders: A Selection, Ed. Ornolfur Thorsson, New York 2000

The Saga of the Volsungs, Translated by Jesse L. Byock, Penguin Books, 1990

The Vikings and their Origins: Scandinavia in the First Millennium, David Wilson, McGrawHill Book Company
    New York, 1970

The Vikings in History, F. Donald Logan, Routledge, New York, 1995

Winter Tales, George MacKay Brown, Flamingo, London, 1996

About the Author

Wayne Gudmundson was born in Fargo, North Dakota, in 1949 and was introduced to the vast landscape of that state from the backseat of a 1954 Chevy. He bought his first camera and developed his first roll of film on Guam in 1969 while serving aboard the *USS Proteus*.

Gudmundson met his wife, Jane, while they were both teaching in Copenhagen, Denmark: they married on July 4, 1975, in England.

He worked for a year at the then newly-formed Plains Art Museum situated in what is now the Rourke Art Museum in Moorhead, Minnesota. Then, as a National Endowment for the Arts Artist in Residence, he was one of the original staff members at the new Creative Art Studio in Fargo where he worked for the next ten years.

Now Professor Emeritus from Minnesota State University Moorhead, he taught photography for twenty-five years in the department of Mass Communications. He also was the director of New Rivers Press, the oldest non-profit literary press in the country.

Gudmundson's work has appeared in eleven books, numerous exhibits, and several public television documentaries. In addition, his photographs are part of many permanent collections including the Museum of Modern Art in New York; the San Francisco Museum of Modern Arts; the Canadian Centre for Architecture in Montreal; the Center for Creative Photography in Tucson, Arizona; the Reykjavik Museum of Photography in Iceland; the Minnesota Historical Society; the State Historical Society of North Dakota; and the Plains Art Museum in Fargo. Gudmundson is represented by the Joseph Bellow's Gallery in La Jolla, California.

Wayne and Jane's daughter, Liv, and her husband, Raphaël, and their two children, Emile and Colette, live in Senlis, France, a small medieval village just north of Paris.

About the Press

North Dakota State University Press (NDSU Press) exists to stimulate and coordinate interdisciplinary regional scholarship. These regions include the Red River Valley, the state of North Dakota, the plains of North America (comprising both the Great Plains of the United States and the prairies of Canada), and comparable regions of other continents. We publish peer reviewed regional scholarship shaped by national and international events and comparative studies.

Neither topic nor discipline limits the scope of NDSU Press publications. We consider manuscripts in any field of learning. We define our scope, however, by a regional focus in accord with the press's mission. Generally, works published by NDSU Press address regional life directly, as the subject of study. Such works contribute to scholarly knowledge of region (that is, discovery of new knowledge) or to public consciousness of region (that is, dissemination of information, or interpretation of regional experience). Where regions abroad are treated, either for comparison or because of ties to those North American regions of primary concern to the press, the linkages are made plain. For nearly three-quarters of a century, NDSU Press has published substantial trade books, but the line of publications is not limited to that genre. We also publish textbooks (at any level), reference books, anthologies, reprints, papers, proceedings, and monographs. The press also considers works of poetry or fiction, provided they are established regional classics or they promise to assume landmark or reference status for the region. We select biographical or autobiographical works carefully for their prospective contribution to regional knowledge and culture. All publications, in whatever genre, are of such quality and substance as to embellish the imprint of NDSU Press.

We changed our imprint to North Dakota State University Press in January 2016. Prior to that, and since 1950, we published as the North Dakota Institute for Regional Studies Press. We continue to operate under the umbrella of the North Dakota Institute for Regional Studies, located at North Dakota State University.